"Your work is going to fill a large part of your life, and the only way to be truly satisfied is to do what you believe is great work...

EntreWorship ®

Re-examining the Intersection of Work, Faith, and Culture

Brian Sooy

OHIO, USA

"...And the only way to do great work is to love what you do. Don't settle."

Steve Jobs

Visit EntreWorship.com for more inspiration and encouragement as you re-examine what it means to work by faith.

Readers Respond to EntreWorship:

"Brian Sooy cares deeply about entrepreneurs and about Christ. This book shows how the two are so powerfully, and masterfully, intertwined."
 — Leslie Bianco | *Author and Founder*
 In the Company of Prayer
 companyofprayer.com

In an era in which we often worship entrepreneurs, Brian brings believers back to the right perspective on entrepreneurship. We create, because we are children of the Creator. EntreWorship hits the core of the things that many of struggle with in our ventures: isolation, feelings of inadequacy, impatience, busyness and more. This isn't just a read once and toss type of book, but a guide that you need to keep close by and read often!
 Todd Greer, PhD | *Chief Catalyst*
 The Exchange (A CoWorking Community)
 Exchange202.com

For my Mother and Father,
who showed me how to
love, worship, and work.

Thank you.

The world needs
people like you:
artists, entrepreneurs,
leaders, disruptors,
change agents, and
explorers who do not
fear the narrow path.

As an entrepreneur who has a living and active relationship with Jesus Christ, I want my work to be full of worship, and to avoid our culture's obsession with the worship of entrepreneurship.

From my perspective, work is worship — but I don't worship work.

I've been thinking a lot about being an entrepreneur, and the believer's role as an entrepreneurial leader. With this perspective in mind, these thoughts and this idea of EntreWorship may not be for you, and that's OK.

I've always believed entrepreneurship is a way of thinking. Entrepreneurship principles are teachable; to be an entrepreneur, you must think like one.

Worship is a way of thinking that can have a profound and deep influence on how we live. When we think first of the One whom we worship, and who he has called us to serve in love, we begin to know God's will for us. It's transformational. To be transformed, you must allow God to change the way you think.

The Apostle Paul challenged the Romans in
Chapter 12, 1-2:

*And so, dear brothers and sisters, I plead with
you to give your bodies to God because of all he
has done for you. Let them be a living and holy
sacrifice — the kind he will find acceptable. This
is truly the way to worship him. Don't copy the
behavior and customs of this world, but let God
transform you into a new person by changing
the way you think. Then you will learn to know
God's will for you, which is good and pleasing
and perfect.*

I believe our culture, including church culture,
has a flawed perspective about work. Business
culture celebrates leaders; the church talks about
leadership but wants followers.

Entrepreneurs tend to be leaders, and

not always good followers.

It's not a fault; it's the way you and I are wired.
In the tension in between live those who want to
live by faith and do work that matters, following

their Lord and leading with the gifts and insights they have been given.

There must be more to the journey of faith and lifestyle of entrepreneurship than prosperity; the drive for success must drive you to want to profit from your business, or all you're left with is a hobby.

We all struggle; we all yearn for success.

I believe the Bible contains much wisdom that is relevant to entrepreneurs. I also believe that an entrepreneurial perspective on the Bible and faith is needed for today.

The last thing we need is "The Entrepreneur's Bible."

What we need is to have a biblical perspective on entrepreneurship and an entrepreneurial perspective of worship.

The intersection of work and faith is what I call *EntreWorship*.

To be a great
leader, be a
good follower.

The Path We Follow Together

If you're going to work by faith,

you need to think about it differently.

I'm not a pastor. I'm a designer, an artist, a musician. I'm a small business owner and business leader. I'm an entrepreneur who loves Jesus.

What's your vocation? What's your calling? Are your vocation and calling aligned?

I'm writing this for you — for when you struggle with business, and when you wrestle with success. For your journey to align work and faith.

50 years ago I would have been called a business owner.

I love God's Word, and I love being an entrepreneur. The risk and the rewards appeal to me.

I view my work as worship — but I don't worship entrepreneurship (or entrepreneurs, or the idea of innovation) as fervently as our culture does.

My work and how I practice entrepreneurship is an expression of worship, solely for the glory of my God and Heavenly Father.

How do you work? Is it solely for you, or to the glory of God?

These verses are worth repeating. Romans 12:1-2 reads:

And so, dear brothers and sisters, I plead with you to give your bodies to God because of all he has done for you. Let them be a living and holy sacrifice—the kind he will find acceptable. This is truly the way to worship him. Don't copy the behavior and customs of this world, but let God transform you into a new person by changing the way you think. Then you will learn to know God's will for you, which is good and pleasing and perfect.

Certain aspects of entrepreneurship are teachable, but much of it a gift.

It's innate, a discipline, a way of thinking. If you're going to practice entrepreneurship as a way to worship, you need to think about it differently.

Giving yourself completely to God is the way fully experience the risk and reward of work and worship.

Not just the part of you that goes to church (if you do), or the time you spend doing service (if you do); but all of you — your mind, body, and spirit — giving yourself to Him as thoroughly as you do to the ideas, businesses, and innovation you pursue every day.

I don't want to worship entrepreneurship.

I want to worship as an entrepreneur.

I want to approach entrepreneurship from the perspective of worship: in humility, on my knees.

I want to celebrate the successes, the struggles, the insights of living a life of faith in business.

I want to live a life of significance and know that at the end, the work I did mattered.

What do you want?

Let's follow the path and take this journey together!

Are your vocation

and calling aligned?

Never Alone

Face your challenges

and celebrate success together.

You may not talk about it much, but you feel it: you're the owner or manager of a business, and you feel alone. As alone as John on the island of Patmos.

I feel it too, and I hate it. I think about it when a business opportunity goes in another's favor, and when business development is slow.

I feel it when there's not enough work to keep my team busy, and when there's too much work for my team to handle. I feel it because I have to be the leader, the visionary, the innovator, the optimist, and the motivator.

Sometimes I feel it when I read an article or book that exposes an area of weakness in my leadership or serving, which causes me to feel I'm not living up to culture's expectations of who an entrepreneur or leader should be.

Sometimes I feel it even though I'm married to my wife and business partner, who has always trusted my ability to be successful.

I've defined my standard of success, and when I don't live up to it, I feel alone in circumstances of my making.

When do you feel it? Be honest with yourself, because you know at some point, you do feel it.

During a recent conversation with a colleague, we both arrived at the same conclusion: As different as our businesses are, and the size and closeness of our teams, we are alone in our roles.

Paralyzed by the weighty decisions around team performance, she feels isolated as she deals with individuals who are impacting the company culture and quality of her company's service.

Sounds familiar, doesn't it?

Our sense of isolation comes from

what motivates us, and where we fail to

meet our personal expectations.

If relationships (i.e. love) motivate you, you'll desire to create and nurture a team culture where everyone performs at their highest, and where our clients are most satisfied.

If respect motivates you (If you define respect by the quality of your leadership or effectiveness in business development), you'll desire to be high performing in leadership or sales.

The thing is, you and I don't have to feel alone. You don't have to let culture define your identity or performance expectations. You don't have to set expectations so high that you never meet them.

You're in a relationship with your enterprise (and by *enterprise* I mean an organization where you lead people, or are responsible for revenue and delivering a service). As in any relationship, it requires love and respect.

Care for and nurture your enterprise, and she will love you. When she feels loved, so will your team and clients. She'll respond with respect and flourish under your leadership.

Sound weird? I'm looking at this from the perspective of Ephesians 5:21-30, where Paul explains the relationship between a husband and wife, and Christ and the church. The principles of love and respect are relevant to much more than marriage.

God knows best. It's not good for us to be alone.

I just need to be reminded of one important truth: What my wife and business partner constantly remind me is that we're *together*.

Together, we face the challenges, solve the problems, and celebrate the successes we achieve.

Together.

Planting, Watering, Growing

Some plant, some water.

As with all challenges entrepreneurs face, growth is always on my mind — nurturing, maintaining, and managing it.

I've found peace in the fact that no matter how much I yearn for growth — how wildly successful I am or how content I must be with modest circumstances — my role as an entrepreneurial leader is framed by the Apostle Paul's admonition in 1 Corinthians 3:5:

...We are only God's servants through whom you believed the Good News. Each of us did the work the Lord gave us. I planted the seed in your hearts, and Apollos watered it, but it was God who made it grow.

You and I are simply God's servants.

We're doing the work God has called us

to do and must watch for His plan for

each of us. Some plant, some water.

In Psalm 32:8, He assures us "I will guide you along the best pathway for your life, I will advise you and watch over you."

As a colleague reminded me: God is the vine, and we are the branches.

God's plan for our business is much bigger than our day in and day out plan.

He supports us so that we might grow from his deep roots and nurturing love.

As entrepreneurs who believe in Christ and who believe our business belongs to Him, we are admonished to plant and water.

Then we must trust God for the growth.

The Hidden Way

God is not in a hurry.

will be the first to admit I don't understand God's timing. From the day the sun stood still in Joshua 10:13, to Christ's delay in resuscitating Lazarus in John 11, time means nothing to God's purposes.

Right now, what are you waiting for?

Is it direction, new business, wisdom for business situations? Is it happening as fast as you would like it to? *Probably not.*

Even when you're waiting on God

for direction, it doesn't always

mean you should sit still.

He does not always intend for you to wait and do nothing; yet sometimes he does, otherwise the psalmist would not have written, "Be still and know that I am God."

If you are waiting for him to reveal the path he wants you to follow, it helps if you're already moving in the right direction. When Israel left

Egypt and it wasn't clear where God was leading them, it was because He took them in a round-about way toward the Red Sea, toward a path they could not see (Exodus 14:17).

When Israel arrived at the shore, they panicked. The way was hidden in the sea, the most unlikely of routes. Moses told the people, "Don't be afraid. Just stand still. Just stay calm."

God's direction to Moses, Israel's leader, was quite the opposite. "Why are you crying out to me? Tell the people to get moving!"

Psalm 77:19 reads: *"Your road led through the sea, your pathway through the mighty waters — a pathway no one knew was there!"*

For the entrepreneur, there never seems to be enough time. At times the path is hidden by the sea. We panic.

Even while we're praying and waiting, we can't be sitting still. If we're moving, it helps to be moving in the right direction. Don't panic.

Whatever you are experiencing now, this time in your life is part of God's deliberate purpose to change you, to mold you, to conform you into the person He has always intended you to be. It's to prepare you for the good works he planned for you.

God is not interested in what your business can do for him. He's interested in what he wants to do through you in your business.

Just as you're guiding your business according to a plan and an intended outcome, God has an end in mind for you. Yesterday prepared you for today; today is preparing you for tomorrow.

Does your strategic plan include God's strategic plan for you?

Why are you rushing it? Be still, keep moving. Make certain you're listening.

Don't panic.

God is interested
in what he can
accomplish for
his glory through
your business.

Tempus Fugit

Be in the moment.

How much is your time worth? If it's as valuable as you think it is, why do you waste so much of it?

The Apostle Paul reminds us in Ephesians 5:16 to "Make the most of every opportunity in these evil days."

Traditional translations such as King James substitute the idea of "redeeming the time."

Our time — just like our minds, bodies, and souls — must be redeemed to yield it to God's use and for God's purpose.

Time is the overlooked gift that we neglect to steward when of all things we are born with, it is the most finite and precious resource we have.

Time is a fixed commodity, 24 hours per day, over a seven-day week. That observation may be obvious, but if you were to keep track of your time as you do with your financial budget, what would be the return on your investment?

The way in which you spend your time may not always accomplish something specific, but in God's economy, your time must be accounted for.

You have been given a lifetime of opportunity, to lead, influence, mentor, encourage, and serve.

We tend to measure accomplishment by what we produced, what is seen, by the number of dollars in the bank account at the end of the day. But is that God's measure?

The verses that precede and follow the admonition to make the most of every opportunity speaks of intentionality: "Be careful how you live. Don't live like fools, but like those who are wise... Don't act thoughtlessly, but understand what the Lord wants you to do."

The way I think of this is to *be in the moment.*

Leadership, influence, mentoring, encouraging, and serving is relational.

Your time is not only to be spent on accomplishing the tasks that align with your calling but also in the relationships that surround you. Your spouse, children, colleagues, and community need you to choose to engage in meaningful ways with your gift of time.

I bet you can think of at least one opportunity you didn't make the most of recently. I know I can, and I'm resolved to be a better steward of my time.

After all, you can earn more money.

You can't earn more time.

Tempus Fugit. Time flies.

Today is a new

opportunity.

Make the most of it.

Busy is Not
a Measure of Success

Invest wisely.

How many times have you been asked "How's business? Are you busy?" For me, it's at least once a week.

For a long time, my answer would be "Yes, busier than I need to be," or something like that.

Now I've started to answer "Yes, I'm always busy — but the real question should be 'Are you busy, and if so, are you profitable?'"

Being busy without being profitable just means I have a hobby and not business.

We have become a culture that values activity over profit. We love to boast about how full our schedules are, or how little time we have as if the activity is a meaningful measure of success.

I'm sure you agree — and you're not the only one.

Valuing activity over profit is like

savoring success without significance.

Profits are the result of intentional investment of time and resources. You can't have a serious discussion of God's economy or basic business economics without understanding this basic fact.

In any economy, you invest with an expectation of profitable results. Many times the expectation of return involves the investment of your most valuable asset. Consider John 3:16; the hidden treasure, or priceless pearl from Matthew 13. These verses and stories are cherished by the Christian faith and familiar to many through shared cultural literacy.

Ephesians 1 and 2 talk about God's immense riches of mercy and grace, assuring us that his investment of his most valuable possession his Son still left him with vast resources made infinitely greater by his sacrifice.

Investment involves risk, and risk is at the heart of what it means to be an entrepreneur.

So what does this have to do with our addiction to activity?

What is your most valuable asset?

Albert Einstein recognized "The most powerful force in the universe is compound interest." The principle of compound interest applies to financial investing, but does it apply to relationships? Not only will a financial investment increase over time, but an investment in people will also provide a return over time.

We frantically spend time networking, trying to see the right people. What if you made the most of every opportunity and every new relationship?

The people whom you meet cycle in and out of your life; approach every new relationship as an opportunity to invest in that individual.

Calculated risk isn't a decision that you can make hastily. We're so free with our time as if we have an unlimited supply. We think we can waste time without considering how we injure eternity. We don't calculate the impact of spending our time foolishly.

We need to view our time and activity from the perspective of "managing our blessings," instead of being overwhelmed.

Where will you invest your time? In what will you *risk* investing your time?

While earning money is important, in the long run investing in people involves the most risk, and carries the potential of the greatest return on your investment.

Time is your most valuable resource. You can always earn more money.

Where are you investing your time?

What "Follow Me" Means for the Entrepreneur

Follow to Lead.

Are you a rule-follower, a rule-bender, or a rule-breaker? Are you a compliant person, or do you tend to be contrarian?

Do you prefer to follow or take charge? Do you think inside the box, or outside the box?

Is there even a box at all?

As an entrepreneur who follows Christ, how do you resolve the tension between leading and following?

What are traits of successful entrepreneurs? Different experts offer a myriad of perspectives: determined, risk-taker, confident, learner.

It turns out there's some strong science behind identifying the traits entrepreneur share.

Research reveals that people like you and me are the most suitably wired to be an entrepreneur. We share traits such as tenacity, passion, a tolerance of ambiguity, vision, self-belief, flexibility, and rule-breaking.

That doesn't necessarily mean that were law-breakers (and if you are, I really don't want to know). Being a rule-breaker means you're willing to see things a different way, and do things in a way that defies conventional wisdom.

I like to think of it as seeing the world in a different way, and following a path that others might not follow.

And if you're like me, you don't like to ask for help, preferring to solve a problem or work out a solution on your own.

We're not wired to follow.

We're wired to lead.

By nature, we're wired to think differently: to be independent; to challenge the status quo, to be disruptive. That's how we accomplish what we do, how we innovate, how we aspire to change the world.

As a believer and an entrepreneur, it's a challenge to respond in an authentic way to the call of Christ to follow him. We're not wired for submission, don't you agree?

Our stubborn desire to do things our own way manifests itself in pride. We don't want to follow, we want to lead. We know there's a better way, and we set about to make it happen.

The best leaders also happen to be good followers. Jesus followed the will of his father, fearlessly obedient until the end. It's easy to talk about it; for us it requires submission, discipline, and commitment to put it into practice.

Your Heavenly Father is here to help you run your business, solve problems, create change. Let him help you, and quit being so stubborn.

Psalm 37:5 simply reminds us to commit everything to him. Trust him, and he will help you.

We like to think we're more sophisticated and smarter than we are. We're smart, we're hard working, but we're also his children. He calls to us.

A good leader isn't afraid to be a good follower.

Follow to Lead.

From Curiosity to Courage

And all the highs and lows in between.

Twenty years ago, I had the opportunity to choose between starting an agency or finding a job. With no job, no health insurance, (and a pregnant wife), the safe path would have been to seek security in a full-time position.

I never had in my wildest dreams considered myself as a business owner or entrepreneur.

I was curious; could I pull it off?

The decision to launch out on my own was like a bungee cord jump: I was certain of the thrill, but not certain if the cord was short enough.

Not confident in either choice, my first few months were split between my rapidly growing business and a part-time professional position within a corporate environment.

Nine months later, curiosity won out and I chose the path of entrepreneurship. For you and me, entrepreneurship is a calling. Calling is inextricably linked to purpose.

The path to courage begins with curiosity; it is rarely straight but offers spectacular views from the highest peaks, and inspiring vistas from the lowest valleys. It is not the destination, but is the beginning of one segment of the journey.

Through my experience with Lifework Leadership, I've discovered the journey of entrepreneurship follows a path which mirrors the journey of Christ's disciples:

Entrepreneurs begin with curiosity:
- Wondering what God's direction might be, and openness to searching for it.
- Asking "What if?" and listening for the answers.
- Moving beyond "how does this work?" to "why does this have to work that way?"
- Asking yourself: "What is my calling?" God wants you to do something unique for His people and in this world through you, what does that look like?

Entrepreneurs respond to the challenge:
- The challenge to follow a different path.
- The call from God to a different and better path that requires a change in direction.
- Responding to the challenge of "follow me."
- Defining the problem to solve; returning to the status quo; not accepting things the way they are.

Entrepreneurs seek clarity:
- With clear understanding and awareness of the direction that God has revealed to you.
- Seeing what could be: a solution to the problem you defined.
- Having the focus and determination to aspire to the vision to which you're called or the mission that drives you.

Entrepreneurs proceed with confidence:
- With unwavering belief that God's direction for you is the way you must follow.
- With unwavering belief in your cause or idea, and the passion that drives you to work for it.

Entrepreneurs are sustained by courage:
- Fearlessly obeying God's direction for you as long as he requires.
- Changing and adapting to make your vision a reality.
- Seeking his will to achieve the impact he has called you to make.
- Courage is found in fearless obedience, regardless of the consequences.

Courage flows from calling and is evidence of the character formed from fearless obedience.

The world needs people like you: entrepreneurs, leaders; disruptors, change agents, and explorers. Counter-cultural revolutionaries.

You are courageous — not because of your calling — but because you believe the One who called you is greater than the challenge to which you are called.

Chance Favors the
Prepared Mind

Observe. Listen. Learn.

Ansel Adams was fond of saying, "chance favors the prepared mind," a variation of a quote by Louis Pasteur:

"Dans les champs de l'observation le hasard ne favorise que les esprits préparés," ou en englais:

"In the fields of observation chance favors only the prepared mind."

Pasteur was a microbiologist, and the scientist who invented pasteurization (the process that keeps milk and other beverages fresh and tasty). Adams was a photographer who captured images of the American Wilderness in the 20th century.

Both were observers.

One of the weaknesses in the culture of entrepreneurship (or cult of entrepreneurs) is its focus on youth as the primary source of new and innovative ideas.

When I graduated from college I thought I knew it all; 35 years later what I know is I'm still learning, with the benefit of 35 years of knowledge, experience, and wisdom that grows with time.

I'm often encouraged by this passage from Proverbs 4:20-27, where the writer of Proverbs speaks again and again of being prepared by listening to, learning from, observing, and practicing what he has taught his child.

My son,
   pay attention to my words.
   Open your ears to what I say.
      Do not lose sight of these things.
   Keep them deep within your heart
      because they are life to those who find them
         and they heal the whole body.
   Guard your heart more than anything else,
      because the source of your life flows from it.
   Remove dishonesty from your mouth.
   Put deceptive speech far away from your lips.
   Let your eyes look straight ahead
      and your sight be focused in front of you.
   Carefully walk a straight path,
      and all your ways will be secure.
   Do not lean to the right or to the left.
   Walk away from evil. (GOD'S WORD Translation)

If you were to ask me, my insights would be: **Purpose trumps passion** — if you are confident in why you are driven to pursue your calling, your passion for it will inspire and compel you to achieve it. Purpose is the foundation for a mission-driven life.

Relationships — Build relational bridges, and make every effort not to burn them. These begin with your parents (and their relational networks).

Character — You can't fake character. Without character, you may be able to create a positive perception for a while; eventually, those around you will see through the facade. Your true character is revealed through your words and actions, and people are always watching and listening.

Words matter — Guard your tongue, because what you say and how you say it reveals your character.

Hustle — If you don't know how to hustle (hard work and perseverance applied over time), you need to learn — now. There's no room in your life or regard for lack of motivation. Your family, friends, peers, and colleagues are watching.

Be willing to be mentored — You won't get the same depth of wisdom informed by experience from your peers who haven't experienced enough of life yet.

The people you meet today form the relationships that will make a difference in your life tomorrow and beyond.

. . . .

What you learn today is preparing you

for challenges and problems you will

face tomorrow.

. . . .

Time not only increases wisdom (if you're listening, learning, and observing); time adds to the depth and network of relationships.

The opportunities you have now will be dramatically different than those that a combination of time and relationships will present later in life. The key is for you to *prepare yourself* for future opportunity, and *be prepared* now for the opportunities that you encounter today.

Listen. Learn. Observe.
And put these things into practice.

No Ordinary Believers

Finding the extraordinary

in the un-ordinary.

prefer to think of what I do in my business is helping humanity, but at the end of the day, I'm just as interested in running a profitable business.

I try not to separate "work" and "service."

In "Three Spiritual Steps to Building a Business," Rabbi Daniel Lapin wrote:

"Your work is one of the most interesting things about you. That is why folks on airplane trips nearly always make the first question they ask their seat mates, 'And so what do you do?' The question is, 'How do you help humanity?'"

Why do Christians continue to compartmentalize their work and their "good works?"

I've been dwelling on and praying through Ephesians 2:10: "We are God's masterpiece ('workmanship' in some translations). He has created us anew in Christ Jesus, so we can do the good things that he planned for us long ago."

In its full context, it's the conclusion to this life-changing truth: you are saved as a gift by grace, not as a reward for how hard you work.

You weren't created to have a day job, and to have a separate way in which to do good works.

Work is a gift. Who you are and what you do, (or are planning to do), has been redeemed as part of God's greater purpose.

My colleague Steve commented, "Always love your pics, Brian... an amazing eye for the un-ordinary." I appreciate the compliment, and his comment made me think about how God views his masterpieces and workers.

We are not surrounded by the extraordinary. We're surrounded by the ordinary, with the opportunity to see the world in an un-ordinary way.

We must have a perspective that is not our own.

You must see your work from the place where God has placed you. Sometimes you are on stage, and sometimes you're in the seats. Sometimes you are the leader, and sometimes you're following.

In every circumstance, you are a participant, not simply an observer. You have been redeemed and created to do the good things God planned for you.

Don't be a reluctant leader or fearful observer. It's time to get out of your seat and get your hands dirty in the ordinary things of life.

Your work, no matter what you do, is worship.

Don't think of it as anything less.

Work is a gift, and it's your inheritance.

Be grateful for the gift of work, and don't squander your inheritance.

Find more hope and inspiration for your
journey of work and faith at

EntreWorship.com
fb.com/EntreWorship
twitter.com/entreworship
instagram.com/entreworship

Brian Sooy is a design consultant, author, and principal of the marketing agency Aespire (aespire.com).

The stories and reflections from the journal of *EntreWorship*® are drawn from Brian's 30+ years of experience as an entrepreneur, business leader, and strategic advisor.

As the principal of Aespire he serves business, nonprofit, and ministry leaders who seek clarity and solutions to communications challenges.

Learn more about Brian's writing and design leadership at briansooy.com.

Other Books from Brian Sooy:
Raise Your Voice: A Cause Manifesto
ISBN-13: 978-1605440293

Raise Your Voice is an Amazon.com top rated branding and marketing book for mission-driven organizations.

Children's Book Series
Luckey Haskins and the Zoo Adventure
ISBN-13: 978-1535283304

For the discriminating:

Typography:

Univers (Headlines and subtitles)

Chaparral Pro (Body copy and quotes)

Aespire follows Bringhurst's *Elements of Typographic Style*.

This book was printed by robots the day you ordered it.

The silky cover is a soft-touch matte laminate.
Feels good, doesn't it?